HEALTHY WEALTH 101

The Keys to Building Generational Wealth in 10 Years

HEALTHY WEALTH 101
by JAMAURY NORRIS

Published by JD Asset Group, LLC
P.O. Box 1512
Jackson, MS 39211

www.jamaurynorris.com/healthywealth

For permissions contact:
jamaury@jamaurynorris.com

Cover by JD Asset Group
Book layout and design by JD Asset Group

ISBN-13: 978-1-7333347-0-9

Table of Contents

Course Introduction 1

About The Course 1

Learning Objectives 2

Healthy Wealth 101: Pre-Assessment 3

Instructor's Guide 4

Module 1: Wealth Mindset "Get Your Mind Right" 5

   Poor vs. Wealth Mentality 7

   Who Taught You How To Use Money? 11

   Setting Goals 12

Module 2: Assets vs. Liabilities "Make Money Don't Waste Money" 15

   What Is An Asset? 17

   What Are Liabilities? 18

   Liquidity 18

Module 3: Personal Money Management "Don't Let Money Boss You Around" . 21

   J's Top 5 Bad Money Habits 23

   Needs & Wants 24

   J's Top 5 Great Money Habits 25

Invest Your Money To Gain Your Time 26

Creating A Budget 28

Module 4: Credit Building "Use Other People's Money" 31

OPM (Other People's Money) 33

What Makes Up Your Credit Score? 34

6 Tips To Increase Your Credit Score? 35

Establish Your Credit As A Minor 37

Effects of Bad Credit 38

Introduction to Module 5 & 6 39

4 Ways To Make Money 40

Entertainer/Athlete Business Owners 41

Brainstorm A Business 42

Module 5: Real Estate Investing "Mailbox Money" 45

Mailbox Money 47

Benefits Of Real Estate Investing 47

Capital Gains 48

Tax Benefits 49

Team Sport 51

Module 6: Stock Investing "Long Term Paper" 55

A Millionaire's Best Kept Secret Hidden In Plain Sight 57

Myths About Stock Investing 57

Stock Terms 58

Dow 30/S&P 500 Companies 59

How To Research And Choose Stocks 61

Online Platforms To Buy Stocks 66

Resource Page 67

Healthy Wealth 101: Post-Assessment 68

About The Author 70

▶ Course Introduction

Reading this book shows there is something in your mind that craves for a change or strength to overcome your life's financial problems, and become better at your finance management. This course in your hand is an evidence that shows your desire to grow in order to live better and build a solid financial foundation. If this is how you feel, then you are not alone. Thanks for mentally reaching out, as this course is a financial training which would help you achieve your goal.

This course will make you financially literate, as you will be able to successfully save and budget your money, spend money wisely, and understand the different methods of investing money.

Let's build!

▶ About the Course

The Healthy Wealth 101 financial literacy course is dedicated to changing your relationship with money by training you on the following topics;

- Developing A Wealthy Mindset
- Breaking Down Assets & Liabilities
- Personal Money Management
- The Art of Building Credit
- Real Estate Investing
- Stock Investing

Audience: High School, College Students & Young Adults

▶ Learning objectives

Before you begin, take a moment to think about what you want to get from this course.

Activity #1: Write down what you expect to get from this course and answer the questions on the Healthy Wealth 101 Pre-Assessment.

My expectations from the course. (What do I want to learn?)

_____

_____

_____

_____

_____

_____

_____

_____

_____

_____

_____

Healthy Wealth 101: PRE-ASSESSMENT

Have you had discussions with your family or friends about building wealth/financial freedom? **YES NO**

If Yes, with who? **FAMILY** or **FRIENDS** (circle one)

How knowledgeable are you as it relates to building wealth? (circle one number on the scale)

1	2	3	4	5	6	7	8	9	10

Not Knowledgeable   Very Knowledgeable

Have you had discussions with your family or friends about budgeting your money? **YES NO**

If Yes, with who? **FAMILY** or **FRIENDS** (circle one)

How knowledgeable are you as it relates to budgeting your money? (circle one number on the scale)

1	2	3	4	5	6	7	8	9	10

Not Knowledgeable   Very Knowledgeable

Have you had discussions with your family or friends about building your credit? **YES NO**

If Yes, with who? **FAMILY** or **FRIENDS** (circle one)

How knowledgeable are you as it relates to building your credit? (circle one number on the scale)

1	2	3	4	5	6	7	8	9	10

Not Knowledgeable   Very Knowledgeable

Have you had discussions with your family or friends about investing in real estate? **YES NO**

If Yes, with who? **FAMILY** or **FRIENDS** (circle one)

How knowledgeable are you as it relates to investing in real estate? (circle one number on the scale)

1	2	3	4	5	6	7	8	9	10

Not Knowledgeable   Very Knowledgeable

Have you had discussions with your family or friends about investing in stocks? **YES NO**

If Yes, with who? **FAMILY** or **FRIENDS** (circle one)

How knowledgeable are you as it relates to investing in stocks? (circle one number on the scale)

1	2	3	4	5	6	7	8	9	10

Not Knowledgeable   Very Knowledgeable

Is financial literacy important to you? **YES NO**

Why? _____

_____

_____

_____

► Instructor's Guide

For those who are facilitating; this course should be as interactive as possible. Real life situations should be used during explanation. Participation is of great importance to the success of this course. Hence, regular interactive discussion and opinions on the subject matter should be encouraged.

The instructor is also advised to maximize the self-revealing power of question. Everyone taking this course has an expectation. Always remember to refer them to their expectation to keep them focused. Questions will play well in bringing the participant to the consciousness of him/herself.

Divide the class into 2 or 3 sections depending on size. Give them room to state their opinion about the topic before starting each module.

In hearing their opinions, do not correct or interrupt them so they can feel safe and free to express themselves. This freedom will pay off throughout the course.

If there will be any reaction, let it be from a fellow participant after the first student has completely expressed their thought.

In a case where you have more than one opinion, do not pick one above the other. Simply state that you understand where they are coming from and respect their differences. More clarity on these matters will be gained with time throughout the course.

MODULE 1
WEALTH MINDSET
"GET YOUR MIND RIGHT"

Aim:

At the end of this module, participants should be able to:

- Know the differences between a poor and wealthy mentality
- Understand how money habits can be influenced
- Know how to set financial goals

Introduction:

Creating a wealthy mindset is a topic commonly avoided in our communities today. In this module, you will learn how to adapt the right mindset by going through different sections where you will learn about money habits, setting goals, taking financial responsibility and how to solve financial problems.

" SUCCESS STARTS IN THE MIND AND IF YOU CAN CHANGE YOUR MIND YOU CAN CHANGE YOUR LIFE"

Assess Yourself: Go over the list of Poor vs. Wealth mentalities. Ask yourself, which **poor mentalities** have you been guilty of adopting that has kept you from being successful financially and in any other area of your life. Also, what **wealth mentalities** do you need to start adopting to help develop a strong wealth mentality foundation?

POOR vs. WEALTH

MENTALITY

Success in Unimportant | Success is an Obligation

Don't live just to exist but live with a purpose of success

Blames Others | Takes Responsibility

Your success is your responsibly. If you're waiting on others to make you wealthy; you will be waiting forever.

Spends Money | Invests Money

You can't eat all your seeds and expect a harvest. Allow your money to make money.

Refuses to Study | Reads & Studies

You can't grow if you don't know, so develop a passion for knowledge.

Attention to Past | Focused on Future

Learn from your past and focus on a better future.

Income-Driven | Net Worth Driven

Companies will only pay you enough to keep you content but never enough to make you wealthy.

It's your job to increase your Net Worth by investing in assets.

Thinks Small | Thinks Big

Never set limitations on your dreams.

If it doesn't challenge you, you're not thinking BIG enough.

Fears Change | Embraces Change

Change is inevitable. Accept it and adapt.

Criticizes People | Compliments People

Jealousy and envy will get you nowhere. Celebrate others and feed off their positive energy.

Waste Time | Buys Time

Time is your most valuable asset. Use it wisely until you own it.

Causes Problems | Solves Problems

You are either a part of the problem or a part of the solution.

Remember, wealth is created by solving problems

Single Flow of Income | Multiple Flows of Income

On average Millionaires have 7 streams of income so if 1 stream stops…they don't!

Work Driven | Goal Driven

Work with the intention of goal accomplishment not for the sake of staying busy.

Pen to Paper:

Which **poor mentalities** have you been guilty of adopting that has kept you from being successful financially and in any other area of your life?

_____

_____

_____

Which **wealth mentalities** do you need to start adopting to help develop a strong wealth mental foundation?

_____

_____

"Your thoughts become your words. Your words become your actions. Your actions become your habits. Your habits become your character and your character becomes your destiny."

As you can see, all success or lack thereof starts with your mindset. Our relationship with money starts young. Our parents and peers influence us on how we spend money and on what we spend the money. In order to build a wealth mindset, we must change our way of thinking and how we approach money.

To change our mindset, we must examine how wealthy people approach life and money. According to Robert Kiyosaki, we must begin having experienced-based learning and developing multiple sources of income. Your money should be invested in things that will make you money, such as stocks or real estate. Expenses should be kept to a minimum.

You should also take time to educate yourself. Financial literacy is key to building your wealth. You must learn how to make your money work for you. You should broaden your skills by learning how to understand the stock market, investing and accounting as well as being knowledgeable in financial law principles and how they might affect you. You can't be afraid to take risks. Failure to take risks can be costly in the long run. A challenge now can pay off big in the future.

We also must leave the mentality of "I can't afford it." behind. Instead, our goals should focus on "How can I afford it?" This allows you to think, plan, and solve problems.

Brian Tracy, a finance expert and author, explains why people are poor and how they can escape it.

1. It never occurs to them to become wealthy: Why? Because they are surrounded by family, school mates, social circle, and role models that are not wealthy. Exposure is essential when knowing what the possibilities are. People who want to become wealthy study, follow and mimic wealthy people and their habits.

2. Many never decide to be wealthy: This is why developing a wealthy mindset is so important. You become mentally prepared, which will make it easier to take that first step in building a healthy wealthier you!

3. Procrastination: Goals are not going to accomplish themselves. Pushing all plans of financial independence to the indefinite future will leave you with no financial future.

4. Inability to delay gratification: Building wealth is a long-term game but not as long as you may think if you can delay gratification and stay disciplined. Top motivational speaker Eric Thomas stated that "It takes 21 years to become 21 years old…so don't rush the process, trust the process".

5. A lack of time perspective: This is the reason we have many poor people. Time perspective is the amount of time taken into consideration when planning day-to-day or future activities. Young people may think they have all the time in the world, but when it comes to building wealth, time is your most valuable resource. And if you don't use it, you lose it.

▶ Who taught you how to use Money?

Whether you know it or not, you are being marketed to every second of every minute of your life. Commercials, logos, symbols, and brands are all vying for our attention and our money with the sole purpose of influencing money habits. Most of our unconscious money habits come from how we were raised. As we get older other factors start to solidify those money habits, whether good or bad.

Pen to Paper:

When it comes to money, write down what you have learned from or what influence each of the 4 factors has had on your relationship with money. *(Discuss with your group)*

Parents:

_____

_____

_____

Friends:

_____

_____

_____

Celebrities:

_____

_____

_____

Social Media:

_____

_____

_____

▶ Setting Goals

Your goals are the stepping stones to realizing the kind of life that you want. Having financial goals and working towards them is an important part of gaining financial freedom. The path towards your goal may not always run smoothly or be easy, but having goals is part of what keeps us on track. Goals gives us a sense of meaning and purpose. When setting goals, make sure you follow the **S.M.A.R.T.** criteria.

Specific: A specific goal has a much greater chance of being accomplished if you have the details mapped out. Details should include your purpose, people involved, potential challenges, requirements, and location.

Measurable: Establish a criterion for measuring progress toward achieving your goal. When you measure your progress, it causes you to stay on track, build momentum & stay motivated.

Attainable: Goals that are attainable include a thorough plan and a determined mindset that will not quit until the goal is reached. Attainability starts in the mind and if you think *you can* or *you can't*…you're right!

Realistic: Your goal must be mentally within reach based on the effort you are willing to put forth. Becoming a billionaire in 1 year is unrealistic if you are just starting your financial plan, but earning a 6-figure income within one year is more realistic, although still challenging.

Timely: Having a timeline is a necessity when goal setting; without it, the goal will never get accomplished. Establishing a time frame on a goal gives you a sense of urgency and prevents procrastination.

Pen to Paper:

What are your financial goals?

Goal #1: _____

Timeframe: _____

Resources Needed: _____

_____

_____

Action Steps:

_____

_____

_____

Goal #2: _____

Timeframe: _____

Resources Needed: _____

_____

_____

Action Steps:

_____

_____

_____

MODULE 2

ASSETS VS. LIABILITIES

"MAKE MONEY, DON'T WASTE MONEY"

Aim:

At the end of this module, participants should be able to:

- Define assets and liabilities
- Understand how assets and liabilities affect wealth building
- Understand liquidity

Introduction:

Your balance sheet can be divided into two parts; ASSETS and LIABILITIES. When we talk about assets and liabilities, there can be some confusion about what those terms mean. In this module, you will learn about assets, their importance, and why you should acquire more. You will also learn about liabilities and how to eliminate them.

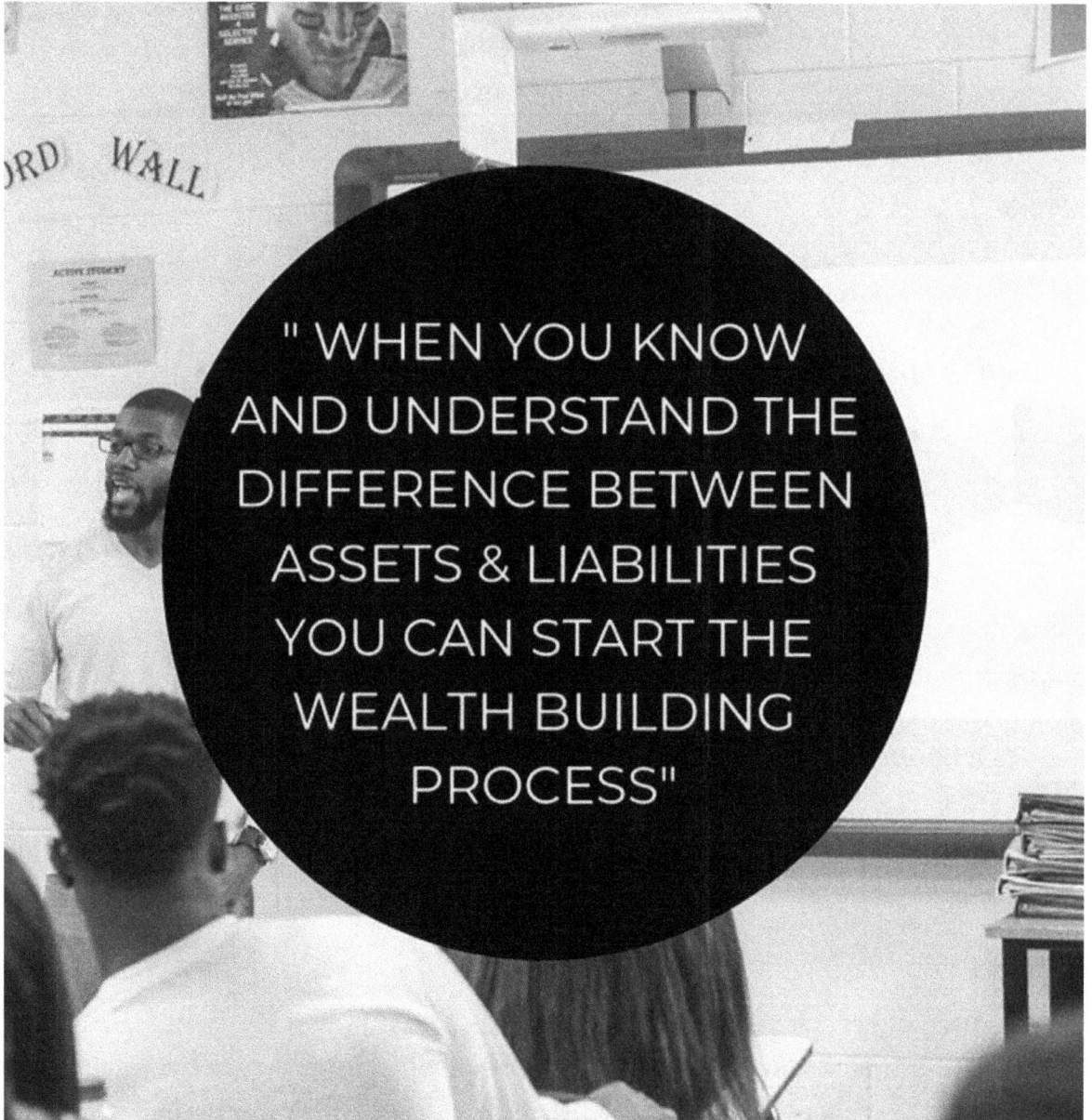

" WHEN YOU KNOW AND UNDERSTAND THE DIFFERENCE BETWEEN ASSETS & LIABILITIES YOU CAN START THE WEALTH BUILDING PROCESS"

▶ What is an Asset?

Assets are things that put money in your pocket. These are items you own that can provide future economic benefits. Assets add value to your finances. The more your assets outweigh your liabilities, the more financially stable you become.

There are three types of assets:

One-time Asset: Something that you will sell one time to generate income. For example, if you buy a house, fix it up, then sell it, it would be considered a one-time asset.

Residual Asset: This is something that you create or purchase one time and it continues to make you money as long as you own it. For example, if you take the house you fixed up and rent it out, it becomes a residual asset because now you receive monthly income from renting the property. Intellectual property such as books, music, and movies are also considered residual assets because once it is created it can produce income multiple times over.

Indirect Asset: This is anything that assists with acquiring or selling the residual asset or one-time asset. For example, your cell phone or computer that you use to help you conduct business would be considered an indirect asset.

Assets are an essential part of becoming financially independent. Wealthy people make it their priority to acquire assets to support their lifestyle. If a wealthy person wants to purchase a luxury car, they don't use their hard-earned money. Instead, they create intellectual property or invest in an income producing asset such as a business, real estate, or stocks to help pay for it.

When defining an asset, you have to make sure that 1, you own it and 2, it has the potential to add value or produce income. If it does not meet that criterion, then it might fall into the category of liability.

▶ What are Liabilities?

Liabilities are anything that takes money out of your pocket. Some liabilities are necessities while others are self-made. However, some liabilities can also be used as an asset. Two main examples are cars and houses. For example, a person may use their home or apartment for an Airbnb rental. This would produce additional income to offset the monthly living expenses of the renter or homeowner. Also, a person could use their car to drive for Uber or food delivery services such as Waitr or Door Dash. This would help produce additional income to offset the car note or gas expenses. Always be mindful when engaging in these activities because if you don't manage it like a business, you could end up breaking even or worse, losing money.

As mentioned before, liabilities fall in two categories, which are "Necessities" & "Self-Made." Here are some examples of both.

<u>Necessities</u>	<u>Self-Made</u>
- Rent	- Restaurants
- Food	- Vacation
- Taxes	- Entertainment
- Utilities	- Excessive Clothing
- Clothing	- Luxury Cars
- Insurance	- Expensive Homes

▶ Liquidity

You also need to understand what liquidity means when studying assets. Assets are grouped based on how fast they liquidate or how fast the asset can be turned into money. The most liquid asset you own is "cash on hand" because it can be used to purchase goods & services immediately, while the least liquid assets are things like real estate because it's more of a process to convert it into cash. Non-liquid assets are classified as fixed assets, while the liquid assets are classified as current assets.

"Make your assets pay for your liabilities"

Pen to Paper:

Look at each picture and determine if it's an asset or liability and why.

Asset or Liability? _____

Why? _____

_____

Asset or Liability? _____

Why? _____

_____

Asset or Liability? _____

Why? _____

_____

Stock

Market

Asset or Liability? _____

Why? _____

_____

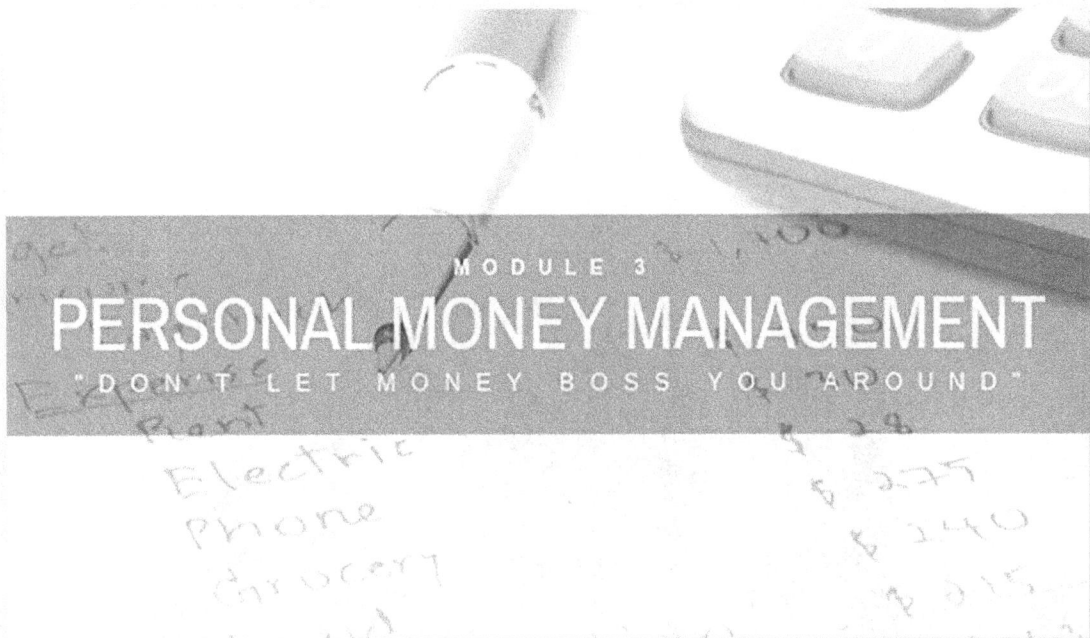

PERSONAL MONEY MANAGEMENT
"D O N ' T   L E T   M O N E Y   B O S S   Y O U   A R O U N D"

Aim:

At the end of this module, participants should be able to:

- Create a budget
- Know the steps in managing their personal finances
- Know how to save effectively
- Understand the importance in paying yourself first

Introduction:

In this module, you will learn about personal money management skills. You will learn the process involved in creating a workable financial plan as well as identifying clear objectives about your personal finance.

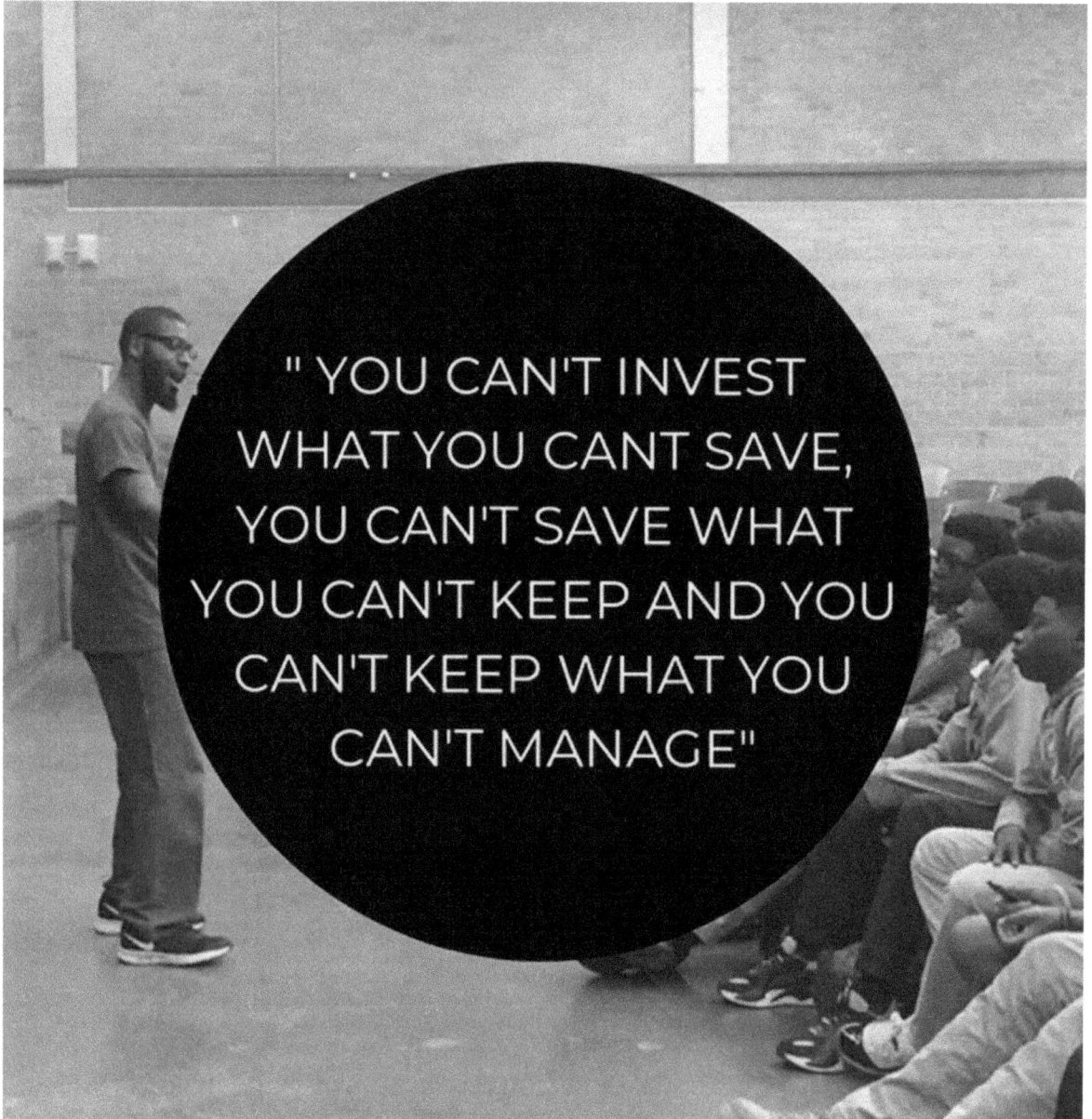

" YOU CAN'T INVEST WHAT YOU CANT SAVE, YOU CAN'T SAVE WHAT YOU CAN'T KEEP AND YOU CAN'T KEEP WHAT YOU CAN'T MANAGE"

▶ J's Top 5 BAD Money Habits

You may have noticed some behaviors that are affecting your finances negatively. These behaviors usually come in the form of mismanaging needs & wants, which will cause you not to reach your full financial potential. So before we get to the good money habits that will help you build wealth; we need to identify the bad habits so that you can break them quickly.

No Budget: Most families don't have a weekly or monthly budget. In fact, only 32% of American families follow a monthly budget. In some cases, it's because it takes the entire household income to maintain basic needs. Keep in mind that those basic needs can also be budgeted in order to help determine ways to possibly reduce them in the future. Families who don't operate a monthly budget generally spend more than they earn and fail to save for the future.

Impulse Buying (SIBI: See It Buy It Syndrome): Many people allow the lure of a sale or "getting a great deal" influence them into purchasing items they don't need. When you suffer from this syndrome, you tend to put your wants before your needs which can be financially detrimental in the long run

"I Deserve It" Mentality: Many people buy expensive items as a reward for hard work or to celebrate an accomplishment. Some people also feel that since they work for the money, they should be able to buy whatever they want without thinking of the possible consequences of that purchase. There is nothing wrong with rewarding yourself within reason, but if you "deserve" it then just make sure you can "afford" it first.

Keeping Up with The Joneses: Many people buy items because their friends or neighbors have those items, and they feel the need to compete. Some people do this to make up for the lack of access to money growing up. Others use it to develop or maintain status among their friends or neighbors. The only person you should be keeping up with is yourself. Don't fall into the comparison trap.

You Can't Say No: Sometimes we can make financial decisions based on the influence of family and friends, which can lead us to spend money we don't have.

That is why budgets and priorities are so important when making financial decisions. Your friends may want to take a last-minute weekend road trip, eat out at

----

"It's not about what you make, it's about what you keep."

----

a restaurant or check out a new movie. If you don't have the money to spend, you can just say no. It doesn't mean that you don't have the money. It just means that it's not in the budget and therefore not a priority. Saying no when it's not in the budget will keep you on track to accomplish your financial goals.

▶ Needs & Wants

Now let's dive into the difference between a need and a want. A "need" is a necessity for survival or task completion. While a "want" is simply a desire that goes above the basic necessity. Wants are not necessarily a determinant on how you survive.

The ability to identify your needs and wants is vital. This will help you determine where to make adjustments in your budget and how to create an efficient spending plan. If you can spend your money efficiently, you will have enough to save and invest. Hence, you will have more opportunity and less financial troubles.

NEEDS		WANTS
Place to Live	←——→	House on the Lake
Vehicle	←——→	BMW
Cell Phone	←——→	Latest iPhone
Shoes	←——→	Jordan's/Red Bottoms

Keep in mind that there is nothing wrong with purchasing the things that you want but do not do it at the expense of going into debt or risking your financial future.

▶ J's Top 5 GREAT Money Habits

Now that we have covered the stuff you shouldn't do, let's discuss the things that you should be doing with your money. Managing your finances is paramount when it comes to securing your financial future and building wealth. As the saying goes, your actions become your habits. In this section, you will be going through five money habits that you should adopt and live by.

Keep your Rent/Mortgage at 25%: Besides taxes, the monthly fixed amount that you pay to keep a roof over your head is going to be your biggest living expense. Keeping this expense at 25% or less of your take-home income leaves room for utilities and additional maintenance without breaking or compromising your budget. People often fall in love with homes that they can't afford. Subsequently, they end up struggling financially or even in foreclosure.

Emergency Fund: While you are executing your financial plan, you need to make sure that you have a safety net. Your safety net is like your financial insurance to safeguard you from financial hardship such as major home or auto repairs, medical bills, or loss of a job. Start with an emergency fund of $1000. As your income starts to increase and debt decreases, increase your emergency fund to 3 to 6 months living expenses. Understand that living expenses include "needs" not wants. Keep this emergency fund in a separate bank account with no debit card access. The less accessible it is, the better your chances of not spending it.

Pay Yourself First: The concept of "paying yourself first" is one of the pillars of personal finance when building wealth. The basic idea is simple to understand. As soon as you get paid, put money into your savings account first. When you pay yourself first, you're mentally establishing saving as a priority. The government is always going to take their cut first, so you have to make yourself a financial priority.

Understand that your bills still have to be paid to maintain your lifestyle, but YOU and your FUTURE are the priority. Paying yourself first encourages sound financial habits and keeps you from living beyond your financial means. Most people spend their money in the following order; bills, fun, saving. Unfortunately, there's usually little left over to put in the bank for saving. But if you bump saving to the front (saving: YOU, bills, fun), then you're able to establish realistic living expenses and set the money aside before you rationalize reasons to spend it.

Save Money to Invest: Saving money will always be necessary when it comes to establishing a foundation for your financial future. They key is to save with a purpose and not just for the sake of saving. Saving money long term will actually cause you to lose money because of inflation. Inflation is when the cost of goods and services increase but the value of the dollar stays the same. Therefore, the value of a dollar today is worth less than it was last year. The national inflation rate has increased as high as 5.6% in the last 20 years, so just saving money in a traditional bank account where you might get 0.1% is not the ideal vehicle for your money. Once you have set up your Emergency Fund, anything aside from that should be saved and invested.

▶ Invest Your Money to Gain Your Time

The purpose of investing is to make money work for you so that you don't have to physically work for it. There are only so many hours in a day that you can physically work and unfortunately, you can't multiply yourself but you can multiply your money. The goal is to invest until your investment income surpasses your salary/hourly income. Time is your most valuable asset. When it comes to investing, time is money. The sooner you get started, the better. Look at the example below. It clearly shows the importance of investing early.

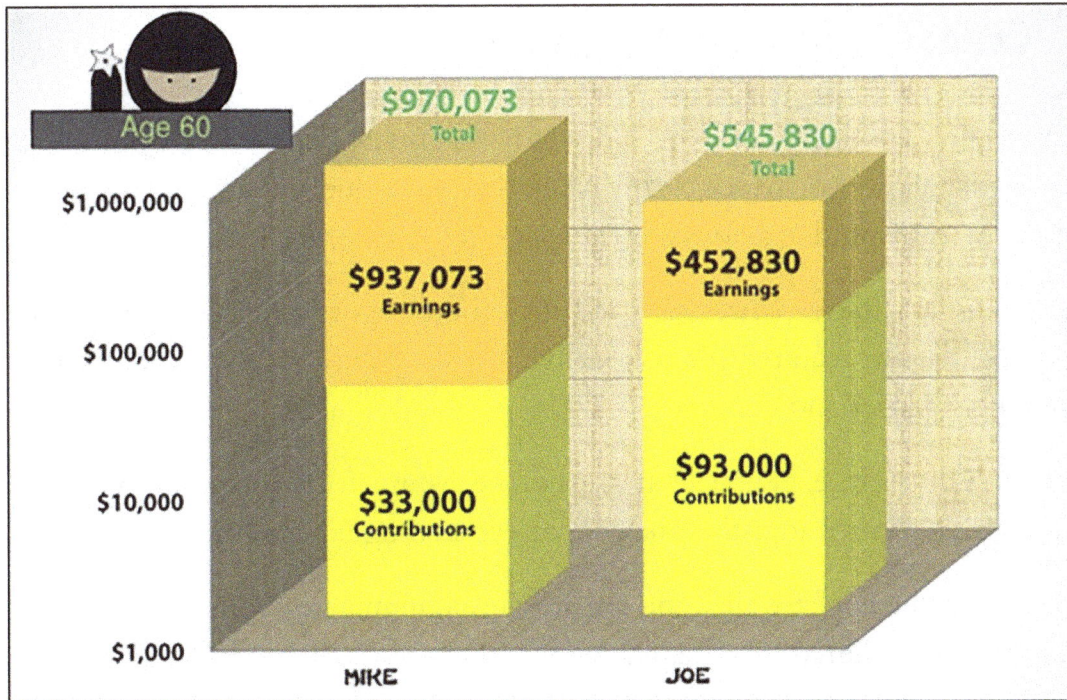

Source: www.personalfinanceninja.com

(This example is based on a 10% annual rate of return)

Mike and Joe are twin brothers. Mike started investing when he was 20 years old. He invests $3000 yearly until he turned 30 years old and then stopped.

Joe decided to wait until he was 30 years old before following Mike's footsteps. He also started with investing $3000 yearly as well.

To make up for lost time, Joe invests $3000 yearly for 30 years until his 60th birthday. At the time Joe started investing, Mike had already contributed $33,000 and earned $22,594 on his investment.

At age 60, Mike invested significantly less (60% less) than his brother Joe, but he made double of what Joes made at the end of the investment. How is that possible? Simple. Mike started 10 years earlier. Remember, time is money!

Create a Budget Calendar

When creating a budget, you want things to be as visual as possible. By putting things on a calendar allows you to see clearly when things are due and what adjustments can be made. Start by putting all of your expenses in 3 categories; Bills, Options & Debt.

Bills: These are the expenses that fall into the category of needs. These are the necessities that are required for you to live. Most of this category will include your household expenses and utilities.

Options: These are expenses that are not necessary for you to survive, and you generally have control adjusting the cost or eliminating it altogether.

Debt: This is the expense that you are striving to eliminate. Consumer debt should be kept to a minimum or eliminated.

Pen to Paper:

Take a look at the Budget Calendar on the next page and answer the following questions based on the numbers.

Is the mortgage 25% or less of the total take-home pay? _____

Are you able to pay yourself at least 10%? _____ What about 20%? _____

If you can't pay yourself 20%, what adjustments can be made in the budget to allow you to do so. _____

_____

_____

_____

Based on the profit you have left over at the end of the month, how many months will it take for you to pay off your credit card ($1,000) and your car ($11,278)?

Credit Card? _____   Car? _____

1: Payday Mort. $1178 Gas $120	2 Daycare $225	3	4 Cable/Int $76	5	6	7
8	9 Cell $55	10 Gym $60 Pandora $11 Hulu $7	11	12 Life Ins. $45	13	14
15: Payday Water $70 Hair $190 Entertain $200	16	17	18 Electric $84	19	20	21 Cr. Card $80
22	23 Car Ins. 141 CarNote $360	24	25	26	27	28
29	30	31 Lawn $100 Grocery $400				

Take Home Pay ($2000 x2)……………..... $4,000
Monthly Expenses………………………….. -$3,324

Profit…………………………………….... $676

Bills		Options		Debt	
Mortgage	$1100	Daycare	$225	CarNote...... ($11,278)	$360
Car Insurance	$141	Hair/Grooming	$190	Credit Card....... (1,000)	$80
Gas	$120	Lawn	$100		
Cable/Internet	$76	Entertainment	$200		
Water	$70	Gym	$60		
Electric	$85	Pandora	$11		
Cell Phone	$55	Hulu	$7		
Grocery	$400				
Life Ins	$45				
Total	**$2092**	**Total**	**$792**	**Total**......(11,778)	**$440**

Visit www.jamaurynorris.com/healthywealth to get your customizable Budget Calendar.

"Those who don't manage their money will always work for those who do."

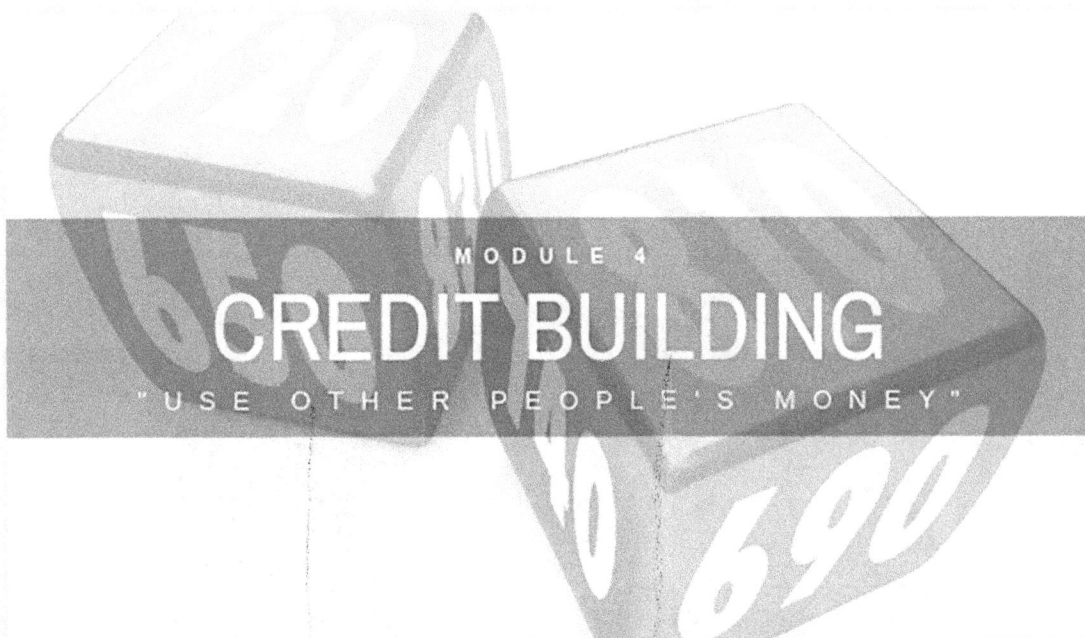

CREDIT BUILDING

"USE OTHER PEOPLE'S MONEY"

Aim:

At the end of this module, participants should be able to:

- Understand the concept of leveraging Other People's Money (OPM)
- Understand your credit score and how to improve it
- Know the causes of a bad credit score and its effect

Introduction:

Improving your credit is a very important step to help improve your finances. In this module you will learn all about credit scores, the process involved in building good credit and how to avoid bad credit.

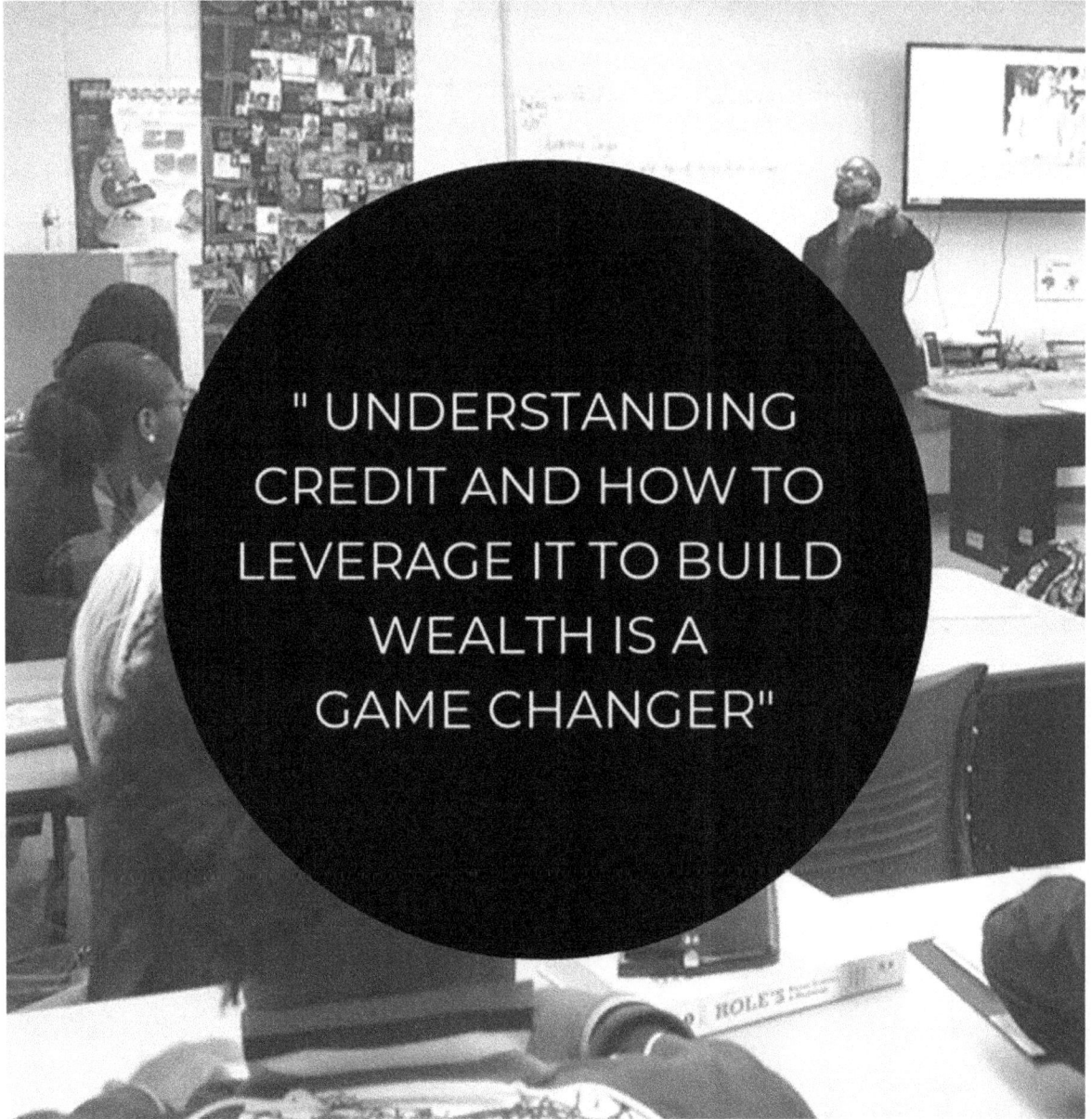

" UNDERSTANDING CREDIT AND HOW TO LEVERAGE IT TO BUILD WEALTH IS A GAME CHANGER"

OPM (Other People's Money)

You may have heard the phrase; it takes money to make money. This may be true, but it doesn't necessarily have to be your money. OPM or Other People's Money is a term used when using borrowed capital to fund your investment. People use OPM for two reasons. Either they don't have enough money to fund the investment, or they don't want to tie up the majority of their money in the investment. OPM is a leverage tool used by the wealthy. You won't be able to work and save your way into wealth, so you will need the advantage of OPM to help accelerate your wealth building strategy.

Example: Assuming there is a property for sale at $80,000 but needs $15,000 for renovations before selling and unfortunately, you only have $20,000 in cash on hand. However, you do have a Line of Credit with the bank for $80,000. You then offer to buy the property for $70,000, and they accept. You then use $15,000 to renovate the property and then sell it for $130,000, making a profit of $45,000. Let's break it down.

Bought property using (OPM)	$70,000
Renovated property with your cash	+ $15,000
Total Investment	$85,000
Sell property	$130,000
Pay back Line of Credit (OPM)	- $70,000
Pay yourself back	- $15,000
Total Profit	**$45,000**

That's a pretty good deal considering you only had to invest $15,000 on an $85,000 investment and tripled your money. That's the power of leverage when using OPM. However, to benefit from OPM, you have to understand how to build and use credit. So, let's get to it!

What Makes Up Your Credit Score?

So how is your credit score determined? There are several factors that are used to decide where you may rank on the credit score chart.

- **10% Credit Mix:** Is your credit diverse? (credit cards, retail, mortgages, student loan, car notes)

- **10% New Credit:** New credit accounts that have been established in the past 6 to 12 months

- **15% Credit History:** How long have you had the different forms of credit? The longer your credit history the better impact on your credit score.

- **30% Credit Utilization:** This is the ratio of your outstanding credit card balances to your credit card limits. It measures the amount of credit you are using.

- **35% Paying on Time:** Paying on time shows creditors that you are responsible

As you can see, Credit Utilization and Paying Ontime are the factors that make up the majority of your credit score. Keep this in mind when increasing your credit score. The chart below breaks down the rankings of excellent to bad credit score. Note: Always strive for **excellence**!

Excellent (30% of People)	750 - 850
Good (13% of People)	700 - 749
Fair (18% of People)	650 - 699
Poor (34% of People)	550 - 649
BAD (16% of People)	350 - 549

6 Tips to Increase Your Credit Score?

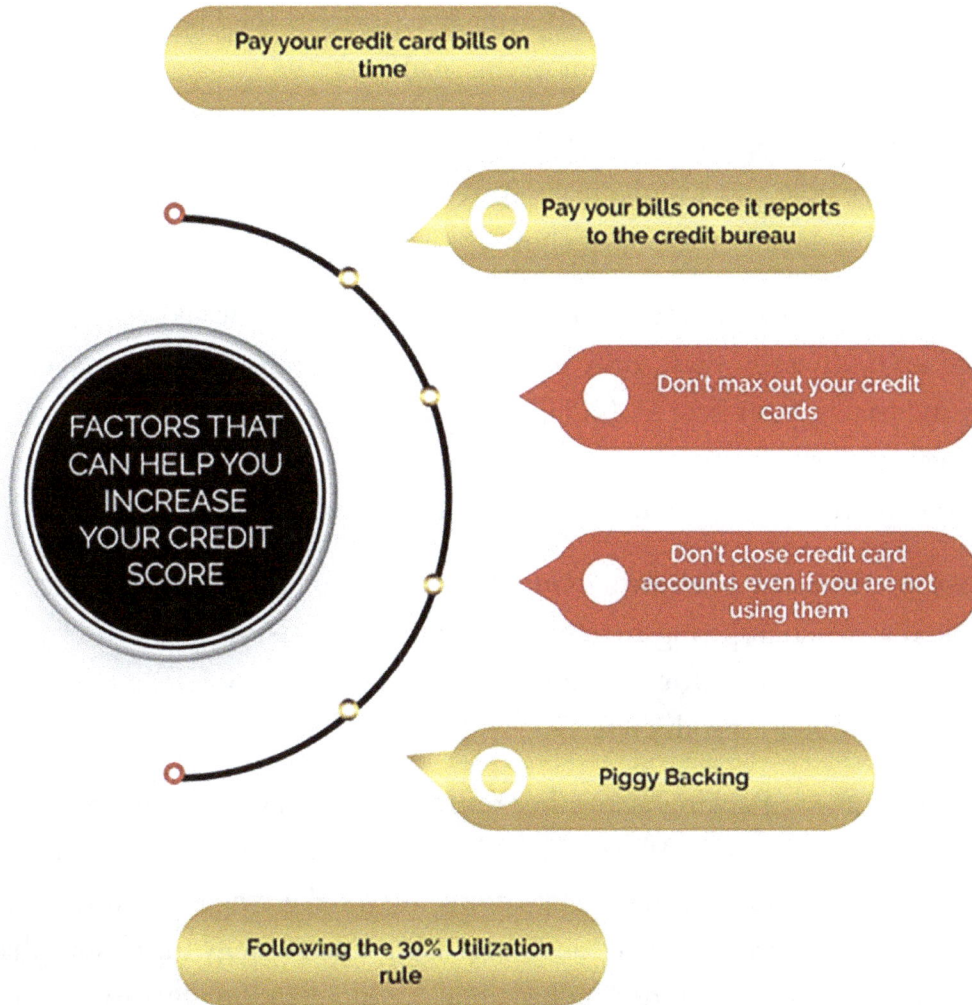

Pay your credit card bills on time

Pay your bills once it reports to the credit bureau

Don't max out your credit cards

Don't close credit card accounts even if you are not using them

FACTORS THAT CAN HELP YOU INCREASE YOUR CREDIT SCORE

Piggy Backing

Following the 30% Utilization rule

Pay your credit card bills on time: Late payments are frowned upon and will kill your credit score. Payment history accounts for 35% of your credit score, which is a big deal when it comes to increasing your credit score.

Pay your bill once it reports to the credit bureau: Don't make the mistake of paying your balance to $0 before it reports to the credit bureau. If you pay your credit card bill off before you get the statement in the mail, your statement will always have a zero balance. This has an adverse effect on raising your credit score because to the credit bureau, it looks like you're never using the credit card, which will not increase your score. Pay the balance off after it reports to the credit bureau, which means after you receive your statement in the mail.

Don't max out your credit cards: Maxing out credit cards makes you look financially irresponsible and will decrease your credit score. Just because you have a $10,000 credit limit doesn't mean you should use all of it.

Follow the 30% Utilization Rule: Only use 30% max of your allowed credit limit. If you have a $1000 credit limit, only use $300 of that limit. This will have a great impact on increasing your score. NOTE: The credit card company will never tell you this because they want you to use as much credit as possible because they get paid from the interest on your balance. I guess they have to make money too.

Don't close credit card accounts even if you are not using them: One of the factors looked at when applying for credit is your credit history. If you close out a credit card that you've had for 10 years, then you just deleted 10 years of credit history, and that's counterproductive.

Piggy Backing: Piggy Backing is another term for becoming an "authorized user" on someone else's credit card. If you are added as an "Authorized User" on a credit card that has a 10-year history in good standing then "like magic," you now have a 10-year history and a great credit score. When using this strategy make sure that the person that you are "piggy backing" on has great credit and a long history of financial responsibility or it could backfire!

Establish Your Credit as a Minor

There are several ways to establish credit even though you are under the age of 18. This allows you to get a head start so that when you start generating income as an adult, you will be ready to start leveraging OPM.

Set up a Secure Credit Card: A secured credit card is a credit card that requires a security deposit. Which means you have to use your money up front to fund the credit card. This method is generally used by individuals whose credit has been damaged or by those who have no credit history at all. One of the benefits to this method is that if you prove yourself to be financially responsible within a year, the bank will usually convert your account to a secured card and give you your initial deposit back. Check with your local bank or credit union to set one up.

"Piggy Backing" Authorized User: As mentioned before with this method, a credit card holder adds another person as an authorized user on their credit card account. An authorized user is someone added to a credit card account and who can use the card to make purchases. I would highly recommend that the teenager becoming an "Authorized User" not be given a credit card to make purchases because the goal is to only reap the statistical benefits of someone else's credit. NOTE: Only use this method with someone you know and trust.

Small Unsecured Loans: An unsecured loan is similar to any other loan but in a much smaller quantity, typically $1000. They key is to put the loan in one account and pay the loan back with its own money on a monthly basis. Do not spend the loan. The only purpose of the loan is to establish a good payment history for the purpose of establishing good credit.

As you are building your credit, you should keep an eye on your credit score and credit report. By law, all 3 credit bureaus are required to give you one free credit report per year at your request. You can go to www.freecreditreport.com to get a free copy of your credit report from each credit bureau. This is ideal for keeping track of your payment history and for ensuring no fraudulent activity is on your report. Another way to keep track of your credit score more often is by using an app like Credit Karma. This app is free and allows you to check your credit score as often as you'd like.

Effects of Bad Credit

A bad credit score can affect your finances negatively, so you need to do everything it takes to maintain an excellent credit score. Here are some of the effects of a bad credit score.

- Getting approved for a loan can be difficult
- Higher interest rates and more restrictive terms on approved loans
- Trouble renting an apartment
- Trouble getting a job or security clearance
- Trouble getting a cell phone contract
- Higher auto and home insurance premiums
- Potential strain on personal relationships

"If you continue to do what you have always done, you'll continue to get what you've always gotten."

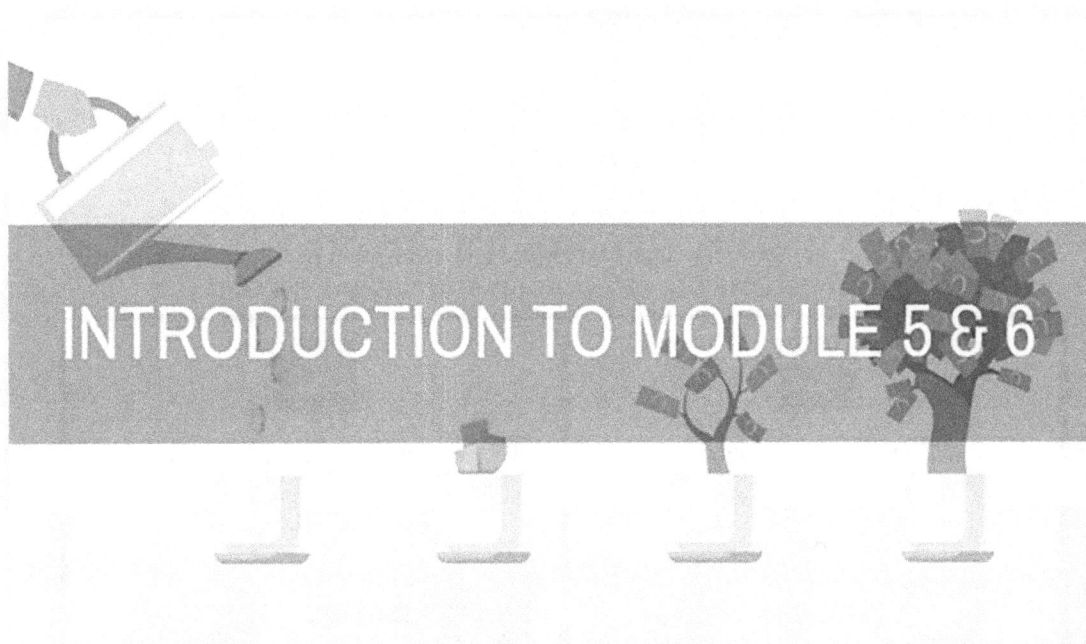

INTRODUCTION TO MODULE 5 & 6

Aim:

At the end of this module introduction, participants should be able to:

- Define 4 ways to produce income
- Understand the importance of multiple income streams
- Brainstorm business ideas

Introduction:

This introduction will help you understand the principles of Module 5 & 6. The rest of this course will educate you on how the rich get richer and how you can accomplish the same thing. Remember, ownership is the key to building wealth.

► 4 Ways to Make Money

According to Robert Kiyosaki, there are four ways to produce income. They are depicted in the chart below known as the Cashflow Quadrant.

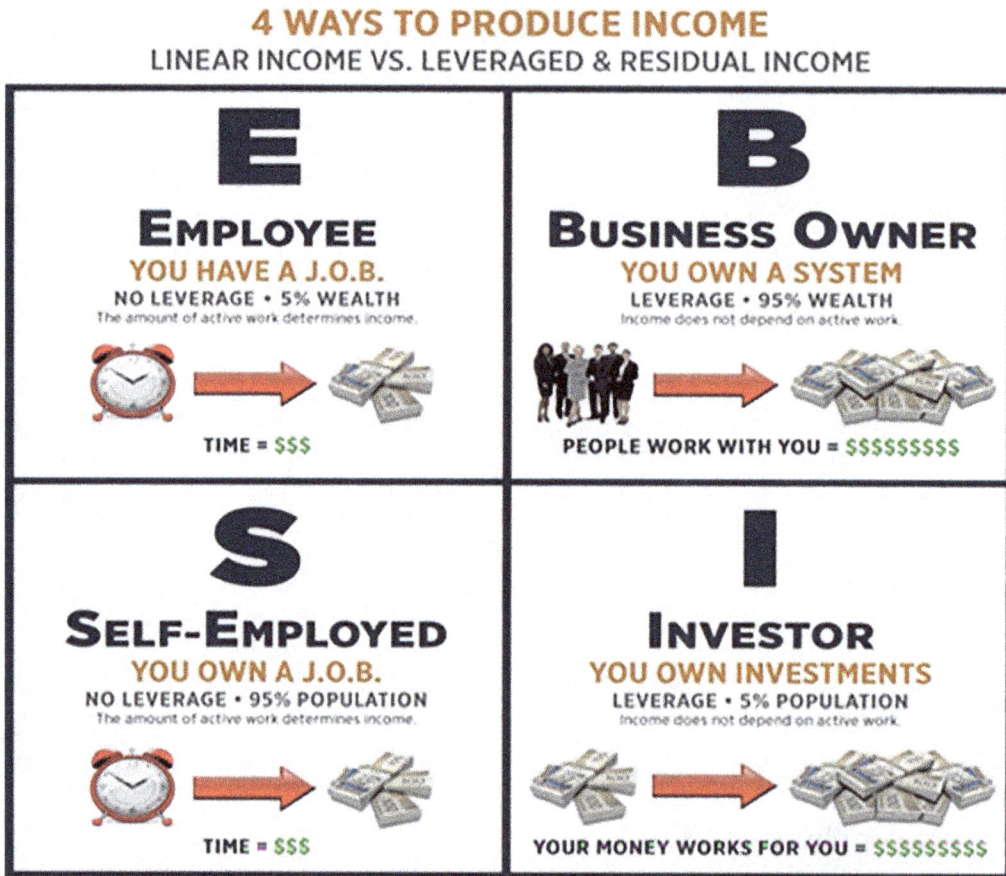

4 WAYS TO PRODUCE INCOME
LINEAR INCOME VS. LEVERAGED & RESIDUAL INCOME

E EMPLOYEE	**B** BUSINESS OWNER
YOU HAVE A J.O.B.	**YOU OWN A SYSTEM**
NO LEVERAGE • 5% WEALTH	LEVERAGE • 95% WEALTH
The amount of active work determines income.	Income does not depend on active work.
TIME = $$$	PEOPLE WORK WITH YOU = $$$$$$$$$
S SELF-EMPLOYED	**I** INVESTOR
YOU OWN A J.O.B.	**YOU OWN INVESTMENTS**
NO LEVERAGE • 95% POPULATION	LEVERAGE • 5% POPULATION
The amount of active work determines income.	Income does not depend on active work.
TIME = $$$	YOUR MONEY WORKS FOR YOU = $$$$$$$$$

The left side of the quadrant (E, S) represents how we exchange time for money. This is 95% of the population but only generates 5% of the wealth.

Employee (E): You work for someone else (i.e., teacher, nurse, factory worker, restaurant manager)

Self-Employed (S): You work for yourself (i.e., lawyer, plumber, photographer, barber, tradesmen)

The right side of the quadrant (B, I) represents how we exchange resources for money. This is 5% of the population but generate 95% of the wealth.

Business Owner (B): People work for you. (i.e., restaurant franchisee, landscaping company, contractor)

Investor (I): Money works for you (i.e., investing in a business, buying rental properties, buying stocks)

Most people start as an employee, and that's fine as long as you plan to migrate to the right side of the quadrant. If Business Owners and Investors create 95% of the wealth, it is in your financial future's best interest to become a part of that circle.

▶ Entertainer/Athlete Business Owners

The average millionaire has seven different streams of income. According to these millionaires, having multiple streams of income is a huge factor in growing and maintaining their wealth. This concept has made many people millionaires, so why doubt it? Having multiple streams of income is the key to building generational wealth. The term simply means having more than one source of income. You need multiple sources of income so that you can still maintain wealth when one of the sources dries up. Therefore, you can stay dry during financial storms.

Several famous athletes and entertainers have become business owners & investors to maintain and increase their wealth. They understood that they could not multiply themselves, but they could multiply their money. This effort builds generational wealth that can be passed on to their children and beyond.

Jay Z: Tidal, Roc Nation, D'Ussé, Armand de Brignac

Sean "Diddy' Combs: Cîroc, Sean John Clothing

Rick Ross: Wingstop Franchisee, Belaire Champagne

Rihanna: Fenty Beauty Cosmetics, Savage X Fenty Lingerie

Usher: Cleveland Cavalier's, Hungry Catering

Lebron James: Blaze Pizza Franchise, Liverpool Soccer team

Nicki Minaj: Lip Stick, Nail Polish & MYX Fusions Beverages

Snoop Dogg: Dog Food Company, Snoopify App

"Employees make a living, while Owners make a fortune."

Brainstorm A Business

Let's take a moment to see if you can capitalize off your skills and talents. All businesses started with an idea, so let's brainstorm by answering the following questions.

Pen to Paper:

What are 3 things that you're good at and like doing? Running your own business is easier when you doing something that you truly enjoy.

_____

_____

_____

_____

_____

Does what you do solve a problem? What problem do you solve? The problem that you solve should fill a void currently in the market or solve the problem better than other businesses that currently exists in your field.

_____

_____

_____

_____

_____

_____

_____

What are people paying for your service to solve their problem? What is the most and least someone may be willing to pay for your service? Find the supply and demand for your service.

_____

_____

_____

_____

_____

_____

_____

REAL ESTATE INVESTING

"MAILBOX MONEY"

Aim:

At the end of this module, participants should be able to:

- Understand the concept of mailbox money
- Know how to invest correctly
- Understand the process to investing in real estate
- Understand taxes

Introduction:

The world has changed. Gone are the days when you could become rich just by working hard. You need to have a financial education and understand what wealthy people do to both maintain their wealth and multiply it over time. In this module you will learn about the principles of saving, investing, and other methods of growing passive income.

" GOD ISN'T MAKING ANYMORE LAND SO YOU MIGHT AS WELL BUY SOME OF IT"

▶ Mailbox money

Mailbox money is another term for passive income. Mailbox money is a very smart way to improve your finances because it doesn't require a lot of time. True passive income is making money at any time of the day without having to tend to it constantly. However, creating passive income does require work but most of it is completed on the front end of the investment.

▶ Benefits of Real Estate Investing

Steady Passive Income: Rental properties produce a monthly residual income that is due at the beginning of the month in the form of rent. If you have a mortgage with a bank, you would pay the bank their portion and pocket the rest. If you don't have a mortgage with the bank, then the rent is 100% yours and thats 100% profit.

Mortgage Is Covered: Even though you have agreed to pay the monthly mortgage to the bank, the monthly rent from the tenant covers the mortgage payment and your profit. It's a win-win situation.

Appreciation: Real estate property tends to go up in value. If you purchase a property at the right time and in the right location, then the property will be worth more than the price that you originally bought it for.

Capital Gains: Capital gains is the profit that you get when you sell the property. So not only do you make money every month for as long as you own the property, but you also make more money when you sell the property. This is taking in consideration that you are selling the property for more than the purchase price.

Tax Benefits: All expenses associated with running your business can be subtracted from your profit so that you pay less taxes at the end of the year. NOTE: Wealthy people pay the least amount of taxes. (explained in Scenario #2)

80% of all millionaires invest in real estate. Why not you?

Scenario #1

Purchase rental property with your savings (3 bedroom/2 bathroom) $30,000

Renovate the property with your savings (fix the property up) $10,000

Total out of pocket cost $40,000

- You rent the property to a tenant for $800 (the amount paid to you monthly)
- You refinance the property for $40,000 (this means you go to a bank to borrow money and agree to pay them back a set amount monthly)
- Your mortgage is $375 (this is the monthly amount you agree to pay the bank)

Pen to Paper:

After this whole transaction is complete, how much money did you spend on this property?

$_____ *(hint: out of pocket cost minus refinance cost)*

How much monthly profit are you making after you pay the mortgage to the bank?

$_____

▶ Capital Gains

If real estate is sold at a profit, then generally, capital gains taxes are due. Capital gains are the profits from the sale of an asset. The equation for capital gains is the sale price of the asset minus the purchase and improvement costs. Capital gains taxes are divided into two different categories; Short Term and Long term.

Short term capital gains are the gains made on the sale of an asset owned for less than one year. These gains (money) are taxed at the taxpayer's standard income tax rate.

Long term capital gains are the gains made on the sale of an asset that is owned for more than one year. These gains are taxed at a much lower rate. (explained in Scenario #2)

Capital gains can come from the sale of assets such as real estate property or stocks.

▶ Tax Benefits

Everyone has a tax bracket based on their income. Tax brackets are used to show the tax rate you will pay on each level of income. This ensures that all taxpayers pay the same rates on the same levels of taxable income. Unfortunately for the employee, the more you make, the more they take.

2019 TAX BRACKETS

Tax Rates	Single	Married-Joint Filers
10%	$0 - $9,700	$0 - $19,400
12%	$9,701 - $39,475	$19,401 - $78,950
22%	$39,476 - $84,200	$78,951 - $168,400
24%	$84,201 - $160,725	$168,401 - $321,450
32%	$160,726 - $204,100	$321,451 - $408,200
35%	$204,101 - $510,300	$408,201 - $612,350
37%	$510,301 and up	$612,351 and up

As a real estate investor, deductions are a way for you to reduce your taxable income, which means less of your income is taxed in those higher tax brackets. Also, long term capital gains tax on real estate sales is only 15%.

2019 CAPITAL GAINS TAX BRACKETS

Tax Rates	Single	Married-Joint Filers
0%	$0 - $38,600	$0 - $51,700
15%	$38,601 - $425,800	$51,701 - $479,000
20%	$425,801 and up	$479,001 and up

According to the 2019 Capital Gains Tax Laws, you can make up to $479,000 investing in real estate and pay 15% in taxes. As a salaried employee, you would have to pay 35% on that same $479,000. NOTE: 90% of tax laws benefit business owners and investors more than employees.

What expenses can be deducted? Real estate tax deductions include the following. These expenses can also decrease your tax burden even more.

- Repairs or Upgrades
- Property Depreciation
- Property Insurance
- Travel Expenses
- Legal Fees
- Property Taxes

- Advertising
- Mortgage Interest
- Office Supplies
- Utilities
- Mileage
- Meals

Scenario #2

Let's compare the taxes paid of a salary employee and a real estate investor who make the same income in one year. (both individuals are not married)

	Salary Employee	Real Estate Investor
Income:	$100,000	$100,000
Tax Deductions:	-$0	-$40,000
Taxable Income:	$100,000	$60,000
Tax Rate:	24%	15%

Pen to Paper:

How much did each person pay in taxes?

Salary Employee: $_____   Investor: $_____

▶ # Team Sport

Investing in real estate can be very time consuming, especially if you don't have the right relationships. It is important to make sure you have a team of professionals on call that will not only save you time but money. Here is a list of the top 5 people that you will need to establish a relationship with before you start investing.

Real Estate Agent/Broker: Finding the right properties to invest in can be very time consuming especially if you are just starting your investment journey. Having a real estate agent or broker on your team will save you time in finding the right properties that meet your criteria. Real estate agents already have direct access to a database of properties for sale. Since they work solely on commission, they will be happy to send you properties especially if they are receiving the commission for the sale of those properties. Let your agent know your budget and they will send you everything within that criteria.

Home Inspector: As a property investor, there will always be renovations that will need to take place, but the goal is to keep that renovation cost to a minimum. A good home inspector will assess the property and let you know what areas will need the most repair. The main areas that the home inspector will inspect are the electrical, plumbing, roofing, and foundation. This will keep you from investing in a property that might cause you to blow all of your profit because of unforeseen issues. A home inspection on average will cost you between $300-$500 and it's well worth the investment.

Contractor/Handyman: The difference between making a lot of profit and close to no profit is what you pay in renovation cost. A contractor with great experience and reasonable prices can be worth their weight in gold. General contractors usually have their own team and can handle most areas of the renovation. If you are a little more hands-on, then you can contract the work yourself by finding handymen that specialize in certain areas of your renovation such as plumbers, painters, electricians, etc. It all depends on the project size, your budget, and the resell value of the home when estimating renovation cost.

Property Manager: Property Managers are the middlemen that handle all tenant communication, repair facilitations, and rent collections. Getting calls at 2 am about emergency repairs can be frustrating so a property manager can absorb that frustration and alleviate that stress. The going rate for most property managers is 10% of the monthly rent. So, if the monthly rent is $1000, then the property manager's fee is $100. If you are new to the rental property game, I highly recommend that you start off managing your own properties. This will allow you to see if it's even worth outsourcing this responsibility. As your real estate portfolio grows, it may be worth the investment to keep your phone from ringing from multiple tenant concerns.

Accountant/Tax Preparer: Accountants and Tax Preparers help you keep track of your income and expenses so that you stay in compliance with the IRS. They also help you manage your expenses so that you can legally maximize your tax deductions when filing taxes. As stated before, 90% of tax laws favor the business owner/investor, so make sure you have an experienced professional on your team that understands tax law so that you can maximize your profits.

MODULE 6

STOCK INVESTING

"LONG TERM PAPER"

Aim:

At the end of this module, participants should be able to:

- Understand stock investing terms
- Recognize DOW 30 and S&P 500 companies
- How to research stocks
- Understand the concept of stock investing

Introduction:

The world is rapidly changing. Developments that took 20 years in time past can be achieved in a day. This speed also affects the financial world. In this module, you will learn about Stock Investing and how to use it as a wealth building platform.

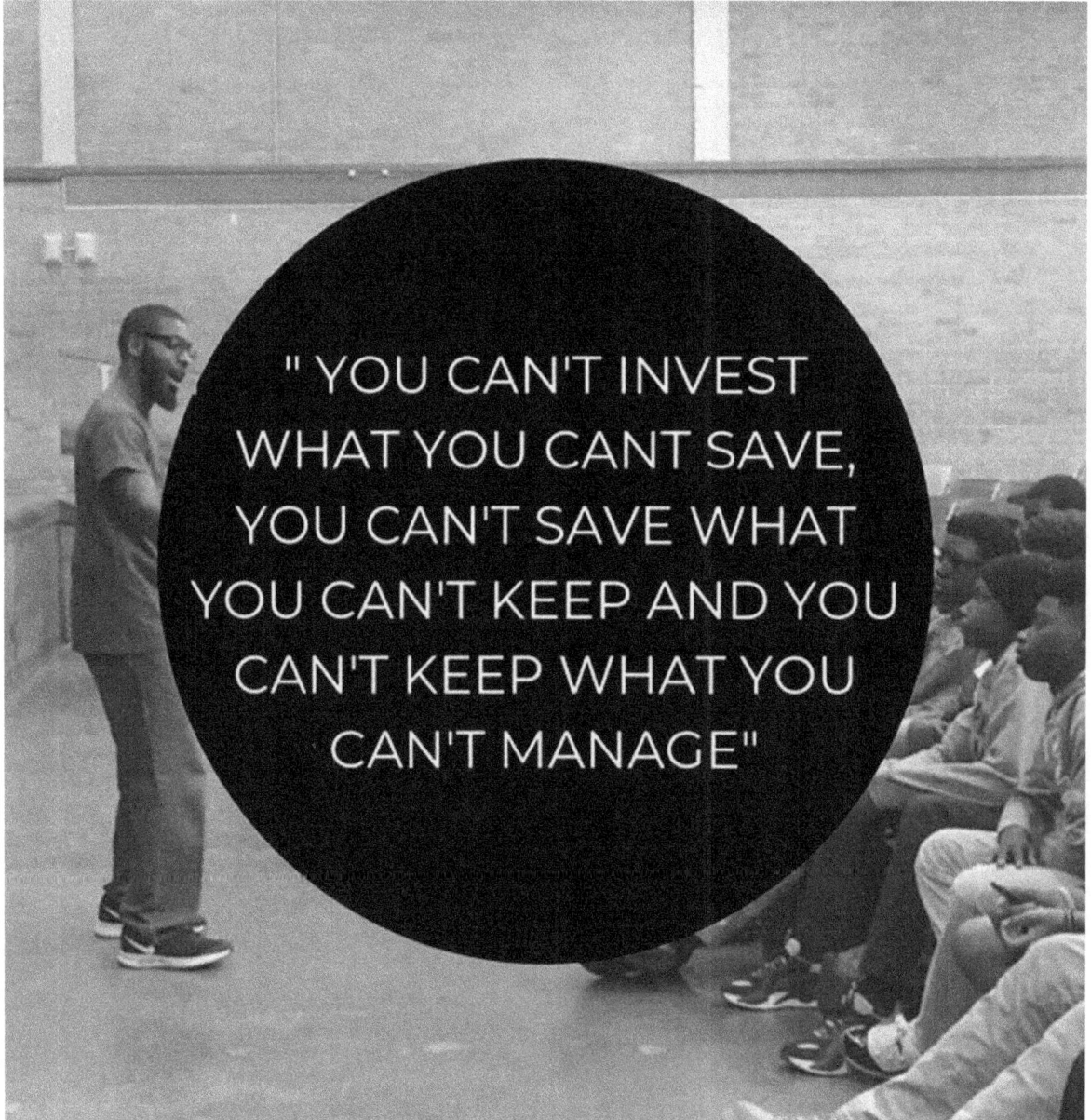

" YOU CAN'T INVEST
WHAT YOU CANT SAVE,
YOU CAN'T SAVE WHAT
YOU CAN'T KEEP AND YOU
CAN'T KEEP WHAT YOU
CAN'T MANAGE"

▶ A Millionaire's Best Kept Secret Hidden in Plain Sight

I remember seeing CNBC on tv in the cafeteria while attending college. I would watch these patterns of letters with green and red arrows pointing up and down scrolling at the bottom of the screen and think to myself, what in the world does that mean? It almost looked like another language, and it was. It was the language of money. I had never heard anyone discuss the stock market, but I soon realized that it was all around me every single day of my life. We spend our money on and consume products every day that are publicly traded in the stock market. I believe that if you spend your money with a company, you might as well own it. As I got older and began to enter the workforce, mutual funds began to surface as the investment of choice through media advertisement and my job via 401k. If you invested a percentage of your income at an 8-10% rate of return, you could retire at the ripe age of 60 with a healthy nest egg. Well, I didn't want to wait for 60 and knew that there were people retiring way earlier than that with more money too. How were they doing it? Stocks! It's funny because a mutual fund is nothing more than a group of stocks, but they sell you the mutual fund and not the individual stock. Why? Because they get paid for selling and managing mutual funds. The only person that benefits from investing in individual stocks is you! This is what the big boys on Wallstreet have been doing for years, and now I'm about to teach you how to do the same.

▶ Myths About Stock Investing

Most of the people I know do not invest in the stock market. Mainly because, like the majority of the topics you've read about thus far, they are not discussed at home and are not taught in schools. Also, the media makes it sound so confusing and scary to the point that you would rather keep your money on the sideline or stuffed in a mattress. Other feelings that stem from media manipulation include the following.

- It's too risky

- I'll lose all my money

- That's a rich man's game

- The stock market is like gambling

- You need a whole lot of money

- It takes too much time to research

Fortunately for you, these are all lies. There is one thing that can resolve these feelings, and that one thing is information. Life is risky, but until you learn you will never live it to the fullest. Now don't go diving in head first. Take your time and crawl before you walk. The stock market favors those who are diligent and patient. Only a fool gambles, but a wealthy man takes well thought-out calculated risks.

Stock Terms

When it comes to the stock market, the main thing you must do is developing an understanding of how it works and how it can benefit you. Let's start with learning the terminology used in stock investing. Here are a few terms that will help you better understand as you continue in this module.

DOW 30: The top 30 revenue producing publicly traded companies in the US.

S&P 500: The top 500 revenue producing publicly traded companies in the US. The Dow 30 is also included in this list.

Ticker Symbol: The abbreviation for a company's stock. For example, Microsoft's ticker symbol is MSFT.

Stock Split: When a company divides one share into multiple shares to increase the sale of the stock. The split doesn't change the value of the stock only the price per share. For example, in 2014, Apple's (AAPL) stock split 7 to 1. This resulted in one share at $645 splitting into 7 shares for $92 each.

Bear Market: When the overall market is in a decline.

Bull Market: When the overall market increases.

Volatility: A period when the stock moves up and down frequently.

IPO: This is an "Initial Public Offering" where a private company goes public and offers shares of its company to the public sector.

Dividend: A portion of the profits given to shareholders as a reward for holding the company's stock. Generally, the dividend is paid out quarterly. For example, if you own 1000 shares of AT&T (T) with a quarterly dividend of $0.51, you would receive a quarterly dividend check of $510.

▶ DOW 30 Companies

Apple (AAPL)	IBM (IBM)	Pfizer (PFE)
American Express (AXP)	Intel (INTC)	Procter & Gamble (PG)
The Boeing Company (BA)	Johnson & Johnson (JNJ)	Travelers (TRV)
Caterpillar (CAT)	JP Morgan Chase (JPM)	UnitedHealth (UNH)
Cisco (CSCO)	Coca-Cola (KO)	United Tech. (UTX)
Chevron (CVX)	McDonald's (MCD)	Visa (V)
Disney (DIS)	3M (MMM)	Verizon (VZ)
Dow, Inc. (DOW)	Merck & Company (MRK)	Walgreens Boots Alliance (WBA)
Goldman Sachs (GS)	Microsoft (MSFT)	Walmart (WMT)
Home Depot (HD)	Nike (NKE)	Exxon Mobil (XOM)

Pen to Paper:

List at least 10 of the DOW 30 companies that you use or have spent money on.

_____

_____

_____

_____

_____

"If you consume the product, you should own the company."

▶ S&P 500 Companies

Amazon (AMZN)	Texas Instruments (TXN)	Colgate (CL)
Facebook (FB)	Goodyear (GT)	FedEx (FDX)
Foot Locker (FL)	Xerox (XRX)	Ford (F)
H&R Block (HRB)	PayPal (PYPL)	Kraft (KHC)
Google (GOOGL)	Intel (INTC)	eBay (EBAY)
Clorox (CLX)	Costco (COST)	Kroger (KR)
Wells Fargo (WFC)	Starbucks (SBUX)	Hershey (HSY)
Mastercard (MC)	Lowes (LOW)	Best Buy (BBY)
Netflix (NFLX)	Kellogg (K)	The Gap (GPS)

Pen to Paper:

List at least 15 of the S&P 500 companies that you use or have spent money on.

_____

_____

_____

_____

_____

_____

_____

Now that you are aware of the companies that you financially support. I want you to view every cash transaction as a potential opportunity for ownership. You will find that there are many opportunities for you to possess ownership than you may have realized in the past.

▶ How to Research & Choose Stocks

When searching for stocks to invest in, make sure that they are reputable companies with a proven financial track record. Do not invest based on a feeling or stock tip that you got from your buddy. Only rely on solid research that can be validated. The best place to conduct free research on publicly traded companies is https://finance.yahoo.com. When starting the research process, ask yourself these 5 simple questions.

1. **Do you use or consume the product?**
   It's obvious from the list of companies that you wrote down on the previous section that you are already a consumer of publicly traded companies. This is

a good place to start because you have already done your research by experiencing the product first hand.

2. How does the company make money?

What does the company sell to produce revenue? You should know this if you are a consumer of their product. If you don't know how a company makes money, take the time to find out or don't invest in that company.

3. Has the stock increased over the last 5 years?

Downloading the Yahoo Finance app or visiting the website allows you to see the 5-year history of your stock. If the 5-year chart is green, it's safe to move forward. If the 5-year chart is red, stop and move on to the next. It's that simple. Don't waste time with companies that don't meet the criteria. See examples below.

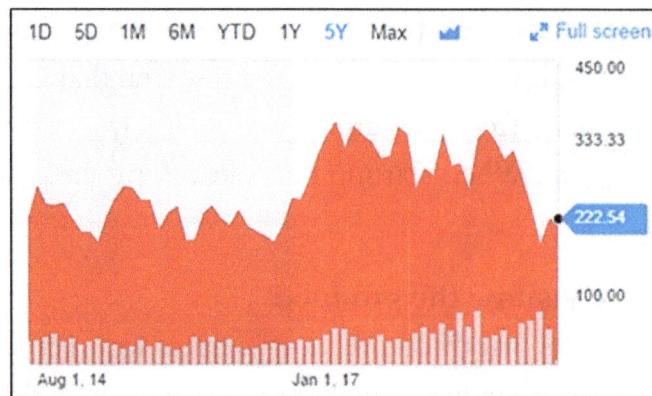

"Ownership is essential to building wealth."

----

4. Has the revenue increased over the last 3 years?

What you are looking for is an increase year over year in Total Revenue. You can find this information on the Income Statement under the Financials tab. See the highlighted area example below. Notice that the total annual revenue increased every year from 2016 to 2019. This is very important because if the company doesn't make money you won't either.

Show: **Income Statement** Balance Sheet Cash Flow					Annual Quarterly
Income Statement All numbers in thousands					
Revenue	2/1/2019	2/2/2018	2/3/2017	1/29/2016	
Total Revenue	71,309,000	68,619,000	65,017,000	59,074,000	
Cost of Revenue	48,394,000	46,185,000	43,343,000	38,504,000	
Gross Profit	22,915,000	22,434,000	21,674,000	20,570,000	

5. Is it on sale?

When a stock is on sale, you will not see it advertised on tv, and you will not get any coupons in the mail like most retail products. Once again, you have to do your research. Check today's price of the stock compared to the 52-week high/low price. The closer today's price is to the 52-week **low** price, the better the sale. See the example below (highlighted in yellow).

153.31 +1.55 (+1.02%)
As of 12:04PM EDT Market open.   [Buy]

Summary   Company Outlook NEW   Chart   Conversations   Statistic

Previous Close	151.76	Market Cap	93.335B
Open	152.62	Beta (3Y Monthly)	2.50
Bid	153.30 x 3200	PE Ratio (TTM)	28.93
Ask	153.34 x 1000	EPS (TTM)	5.30
Day's Range	150.72 - 153.56	Earnings Date	Aug 15, 2019
52 Week Range	124.46 - 292.76	Forward Dividend & Yield	0.64 (0.42%)
Volume	3,195,683	Ex-Dividend Date	2019-05-30
Avg. Volume	11,696,468	1y Target Est	183.42
Analyst Recommendation by Argus Research	BUY	Fair Value View details	Undervalued

This would be a good example of a stock that is on sale. The 52 Week Range is 124.46 – 292.76. This means that its highest price year to date was $292.76 and its lowest price year to date was $124.46. As of today, the current price of $153.31 is closer to its 52-week low, which makes it a great buy. You must understand that the sale price is subjective and determined by you. It just depends on what price you are willing to pay and how patient you are. While you are waiting, create a watchlist in your yahoo finance app or online of those companies that you may be interested in owning in the future.

Pen to Paper:

Time to do some research! Take the company **Netflix (NFLX)** and answer the questions below using Yahoo Finance.

1. Do you use or consume the product? If so, how often?

_____

_____

2. How does the company make money?

_____

_____

3. Has the stock increased over the last 5 years? If so, what was the price 5 years ago and what is the current price?

_____

_____

4. Has the revenue increased over the last 3 years? If so, what were the total revenues for the last 3 years?

_____

_____

5. In your opinion, Is it on sale? _____

What is the 52 Week Range? _____

As mentioned before, time is your greatest asset. When you mix investing with the value of time, you can become very wealthy. Look at what 5 years can do when you invest in the right companies. Let's take a look at Facebook & Netflix. Between both companies, you have a 58% to 127% annual return on your money. No mutual fund will ever come close to that, and that is why wealthy people invest in the stock market.

Facebook (FB)

      5 years ago: **$65** – Today's Price: **$191**

      Invest **$1000** five years ago = **$2,900** value today

      Invest **$10,000** five years ago = **$29,000** value today

      Invest **$100,000** five years ago = **$290,000** value today

Netflix (NFLX)

      5 years ago: **$58** – Today's Price: **$369**

      Invest **$1000** five years ago = **$6,300** value today

      Invest **$10,000** five years ago = **$63,000** value today

      Invest **$100,000** five years ago = **$630,000** value today

NOTE: Stock prices reflect the time that the course was written.

Online Platforms to Buy Stocks

When you are ready to start buying stocks, you will need to set up an online brokerage account. Setting up a brokerage account is just like filling out an online application, and it only takes about 10 minutes. Here are a few brokerage recommendations listed below. They all have different levels of service that they provide and different fees. Do your homework to see what works best for you. If you want to practice buying stocks without using real money, go to www.investopedia.com/simulator and set up a demo account. On this platform, you can buy and trade stocks in the real market with $100,000 in demo money.

Online Brokerage Companies

TD Ameritrade: www.tdameritrade.com

E*TRADE: https://us.etrade.com/home

Ally: https://www.ally.com/invest/

Robinhood: https://www.robinhood.com/

▶ Resource Page

PODCAST

- The Secret to Success
- Trading Stocks Made Easy
- Side Hustle School

APPS

- Yahoo Finance: Stock Research
- Ameritrade: Purchase Stocks
- Mint: Budgeting
- Credit Karma: Credit Score
- Smart Receipts: Expense Tracking

WEBSITES

- www.tdameritrade.com
- www.investopedia.com
- www.finance.yahoo.com
- www.jamaurynorris.com/healthywealth

BOOKS

- Cashflow Quadrant, by Robert Kiyosaki
- The Millionaire Next Door, by Thomas J Stanley
- Think & Grow Rich: A Black Choice, by Dennis Kimbro
- Rich Dad Poor Dad, by Robert Kiyosaki

Healthy Wealth 101: POST-ASSESSMENT

Now that you have completed the course, complete the questions based on your newly acquired knowledge.

How has your mindset changed about money? (circle one number on the scale)

1	2	3	4	5	6	7	8	9	10

Same   Improved Some   Improved Greatly

Do you have a better understanding of assets and liabilities? (circle one number on the scale)

1	2	3	4	5	6	7	8	9	10

Not at all   Somewhat   Absolutely

Do you feel better prepared to manage and budget your money? (circle one number on the scale)

1	2	3	4	5	6	7	8	9	10

Not at all   Somewhat   Absolutely

Do you feel better prepared to build your credit? (circle one number on the scale)

1	2	3	4	5	6	7	8	9	10

Not at all   Somewhat   Absolutely

Do you have a better understanding of how to invest in real estate? (circle one number on the scale)

1	2	3	4	5	6	7	8	9	10

Not at all   Somewhat   Absolutely

Do you have a better understanding of how to invest in stocks? (circle one number on the scale)

1	2	3	4	5	6	7	8	9	10

Not at all   Somewhat   Absolutely

Overall, do you feel better prepared financially because of this course? (circle one number on the scale)

1	2	3	4	5	6	7	8	9	10

Not at all   Somewhat   Absolutely

Now that you have a better understanding of how money works, what do you intend doing with the information?

_____

_____

_____

_____

_____

_____

_____

_____

_____

_____

_____

_____

_____

_____

_____

_____

_____

About the Author

I spent 16 years educating myself just to get a job but never learned how to **manage, invest, or build wealth** from the money I brought home.

The only wealthy people I would often see were the athletes and entertainers on television. My only problem was that I couldn't sing, act and I wasn't athletic. Also, athletes and entertainers only make up 1% of the 11 million current millionaires in the United States. So apparently there had to be other ways to build wealth. During my adulthood, I started to read and research anything that had to do with money, investing, and entrepreneurship.

The moment I began to see success through knowledge and application, I felt the urge to **educate others and break the cycle of poor financial literacy** within my community.

Like me, most kids were graduating from high school and college without the basic financial skills needed to excel in life.

In order to break the cycle of lack of financial literacy in our schools, colleges and with young adults I understood that I would have to be a **part of the solution** and not let the problem perpetuate.

The foundation of economic empowerment starts with financial literacy, and if you don't know, you can't grow.

To your financial success,

JaMaury Norris

For booking: Contact us at www.jamaurynorris.com